SCOTLAND IN OLD PHOTOGRAPHS

DUNDEE AT WORK

JANICE MURRAY

Budding
BOOKS

D0300020

A Budding Book

First published in 1995 by Alan Sutton
Publishing Limited

This edition published in 1999 by Budding Books,
an imprint of Sutton Publishing Limited
Phoenix Mill · Thrupp · Stroud · Gloucestershire
GL5 2BU

Copyright © Dundee Art Galleries and Museums,
1995

A catalogue record for this book is available from
the British Library

ISBN 1-84015-117-X

Typesetting and origination by
Sutton Publishing Limited.
Printed in Great Britain by
Redwood Books, Trowbridge, Wiltshire

To Tom and Stephen

Contents

Theresa McCracken (right) and friend at their looms, 1940s.

Introduction

A good historic photograph is both a record and an evocation of the past. There are many things in the following pages which will stir familiar memories but also things which will seem strange to modern eyes. The photographs in this book broadly cover the period from the 1860s to the 1960s. Before 1860 there were few cameras in Dundee and few photographs of the city at all survive before that date. The 1960s, it is sometimes disconcerting to realise, are now sufficiently distant to be classed as 'old'.

The 1960s also forms a watershed in another way. Most of the people here are pictured making things, usually in factories, busy at the bench, conveyor-belt or loom. There are fewer images which show people in offices and shops. The last twenty-five years have seen a major shift in employment with fewer people working in manufacturing and more people working in service industries.

It is important to remember, however, that if the world of work in Dundee differs now from then, Dundee also differed substantially from almost any other Scottish city in its economic make-up and patterns of employment.

Unlike Edinburgh and Aberdeen and more so even than Glasgow, Dundee was a solidly manufacturing city. Moreover its manufacturing was based around one industry, textiles, which employed almost half the population before the Second World War. Like all single-industry economies Dundee went through cycles of boom and depression, culminating in the long depression of the 1930s when some 35 per cent of the working population and 39 per cent of those involved in textiles were unemployed.

Work often defines the character and development of a place and this is certainly true of Dundee. The dominance of manufacturing led to the stunting of the service sector. The city remained overwhelmingly working class with only a tiny middle class population, many of whom worked in education. The textile industries provided low paid jobs for large numbers of women and children. Historically, Dundee had a higher proportion of working women and working mothers than any other Scottish city in an era when married women were expected to stay at home.

As always with any collection of photographs there are glaring omissions in this compilation which reflect the pre-occupations of the photographer, or in this case, the institutional collector. There are few photographs of unpaid domestic workers, nor significantly are there many photographs of the unemployed, or of the children that we know were a constant feature of Dundee mills before the First World War.

The museum collections' strengths are also reflected in these pages. Only a proportion of our excellent textile and shipbuilding collections are shown here while the inclusion of our early military collections reveals a hidden aspect of the late Victorian city which is little known. Similarly, people will search in vain for images of the whaling trade or of Dundee's port, not because the museum does not have any, but because such riches as we do have deserve another book to themselves.

Formed over a number of years from the museum's foundation in 1873, it is only in the last decade that the photography collections have been considerably enlarged and fully documented. They are an invaluable resource for researchers, schoolchildren and the public at large. Catalogues of the photographs can be consulted by appointment with the Human History Section and copy prints can be supplied for a small charge.

Janice Murray
Dundee Art Galleries
and Museums

THE STAFF OF LIFE

*Berry pickers in the Carse of Gowrie. At the beginning of this century there were large jam
manufacturers not just in Dundee but in Coupar Angus, Newtyle and Blairgowrie as well.*

Dundee is bounded on three sides by countryside and originally the city's rural hinterland was also its larder. There was always an abundance of agricultural produce from the fertile Carse of Gowrie in Dundee's markets, while its coastal position meant that fresh fish were sold on the streets within hours of landing. Imported foods and drink were brought into the docks.

Up until the Second World War the physical and emotional divide between city and country was much smaller than today. City-dwellers commonly spent their 'holidays' berry-picking in summer or tattie-picking in the autumn.

Local agricultural produce was processed in the city's factories, the most famous of which was the jam maker and confectioner, James Keiller & Son – Britain's biggest confectionery firm by the end of the 1860s.

Rising living standards in Britain in the last quarter of the 19th century produced a greater demand for food beyond the basic necessities. The factory-produced food sector, like the jams and sweets of Keiller's, expanded and with this expansion came a growth in retailing.

A new type of shop appeared – aimed at the largest market of all, the working classes, and selling huge amounts of industrially produced foodstuffs at reasonable prices. Shops which followed this trend were incredibly successful. Dundee's own retailing pioneer was William Low, who joined his brother's grocery shop in Hunter Street in 1870 and built up a business of 64 branches stretching from Dingwall to Hawick by 1900. The Wm Low chain had its headquarters in Dundee throughout its history, until it was taken over by Tesco in 1994.

Threshing by steam engine at Gleigs farm, Woodhaven, Fife, c. 1920.

Harvesting at Westgreen, 1923.

Mr and Mrs McDonald, their daughter and Italian prisoners of war, who were working the land at Pitkerro Nurseries, Baldovie Toll, Dundee, 1944.

Robert Fenwick, farrier of the Victoria Shoeing Forge, Dock Street, with his prize-winning display of farrier's tools, horses' shoes and hooves. The collection was donated to the museum in 1942.

Fishwives selling in the Greenmarket. The wives of fishermen from up and down the coast brought their catch to sell in the city centre.

Food-stalls at Shore Terrace, *c.* 1910.

Discharging, weighing and wagoning sugar, Dundee docks, 1936.

Thomas Foote, grocer and provisions dealer outside his shop in Flights Lane, Lochee, *c.* 1910. By the end of the 19th century grocers commonly stocked both provisions (bacon, ham, eggs, dairy produce) and groceries (tea, coffee, spices, dried fruit). The latter had once been expensive luxuries reserved for the tables of the wealthy.

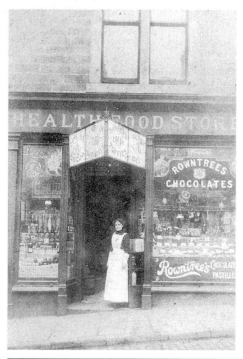

Mrs Margaret Thomson stands at the door of her shop at 290 Hilltown.

Wm Low and Co., 304 Perth Road. Successful grocery chains like Wm Low's which sold to working-class customers started off by selling only a narrow range of foods at keen prices. Imported produce such as the Canadian Cheddar advertised in the window was definitely aimed at the cheaper end of the market.

Head office employees of Wm Low, 1914. At the beginning of the century, women working in the retail sector tended to be concentrated in trades like drapery or to work in particular departments of large businesses, especially cashiering and book keeping. Behind the counter they remained a minority until after the Second World War.

Wm Low's head office was in Blackness Road until 1959 when it moved to Bellfield Street.

Kydd Brothers' shop in the Wellgate. Henry Clunie, message boy aged 14, stands on the left. Message boys on large heavy bikes with baskets frequently rode miles to deliver customers' orders.

The staff of the Dundee Eastern Co-operative Society, Strathmore Avenue, 1930s. William Davidson, manager, is on the right inside the door, James Young on the left of the door and Wood Allen on the extreme right. Founded in 1863, the Dundee Eastern was the largest of the Co-operative Societies in the city and ran a drapery and bakery as well as a grocery business.

Wm Low's Broughty Ferry foodstore, 1960s. The first grocery chains in Britain to turn to self-service were some Co-operative Societies and Tesco in about 1950. Wm Low's took on the concept in 1958 and brought it to Dundee in the early 1960s.

The premises of T. Anderson, butchers, 146a Hilltown. 'High Class' usually meant the butcher sold mostly British rather than imported refrigerated meat. Apprentice butcher Richard McLeod is on the right.

Lecturer Frederick Leitch takes a tea tasting class for grocery apprentices at Dundee College of Commerce, 1935.

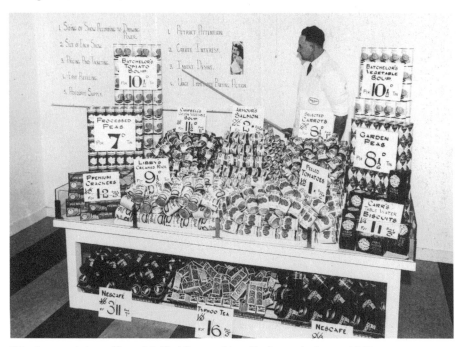

Wm Low training officer, Mr Keddie, teaching display techniques, 1950s.

A view of the sugar boiling room in Lindsay and Low's preserve and confectionery factory at Carolina Port, *c.* 1915. Lindsay and Low was formed in 1871 by two grocers, William Lindsay and James Low, who had a ready outlet for their goods in James and William Low's grocery business. In 1879 James Low left the retail side to concentrate on his manufacturing concern.

Keiller's factory entrance, Albert Square, Dundee, decorated to welcome King George V, 10 July 1914.

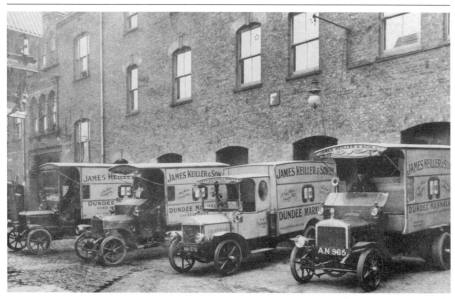

Keiller's delivery lorries parked outside the factory in Albert Square. Keiller's were taken over by Crosse and Blackwell in 1922 and in turn by Nestlé in 1961. Between the wars Keiller's bakery at Mains Loan, Maryfield employed about 140 people, supplying 23 shops and 8 restaurants in the city. After the Second World War, new preserves and Toblerone chocolate factories were built on the Mains Loan site.

Bessie Dewar explains sweetie making to John Strachey MP, Minister for Food, on his visit to Keiller's factory, 7 March 1949.

Coopers from the firm of Galloway & Co., making a giant 2,000 gallon spirit blending vat for James Watson distillers. Whisky firms in Dundee distilled in the Highlands and blended and bottled their products in the city.

The bottling floor in the whisky bond of Alexander Stewart & Son, in the Seagate, *c.* 1925. The firm also had premises in Castle Street, Exchange Street, and the no. 2 Custom House. Distillers of the famous 'Cream of the Barley' they supplied amongst others the Houses of Parliament, the Admiralty, War Office, the Belgian Government and the King of Spain.

Traction engine delivery vehicle of James Watson & Co., Watson's Bond, Seagate, Dundee.

William McGovern (right) and Johnnie Rae (centre), bar staff at the Windmill Bar, 113 Hilltown, 1930s.

Publican Charles Strachan, Frederick Mitchell and Lennox Dale outside Strachan's, 32–4 Smalls Wynd. There was a Strachan's pub in Smalls Wynd from the 1850s to 1957. University buildings now stand on the site.

Staff at Ballingall's brewery sample the product, 1950s. Ballingall's, with their Park and Pleasance Breweries off the Lochee Road, were Dundee's largest brewers. Although there had been brewing conducted at the Pleasance brewery since the middle of the 18th century, the business owed its modern success to Hugh Ballingall who ran the firm from the 1860s. Brewing ceased at Ballingall's in 1964.

The Fugaccia family gutting fish at the back of the Popular Café fish and chip shop, 14 St Andrews Street, 1939. With more than half of all women in Dundee going out to work between the wars, there was a demand for cheap, nourishing food in the city.

Proprietor Giuseppina Gierelo, Christina Notrangelo and Maria Paesano at their fish and chip shop in Baffin Street, 1967. Italians dominated the fish and chip trade in the city from the 1920s. In 1967 52 out of 63 shops were owned by families of Italian descent.

Section Two

TEXTILES

Beaming up a loom, Nelson Street Works, c. 1911.

In the 16th century, the trading of such things as fleeces and woollen and linen goods made Dundee the second richest city in Scotland. In the 18th century it became a distribution centre for the coarse linens which were produced in Angus, and in the 19th century it became Juteopolis, the world centre for the coarse cloth which backed carpets, bagged food, upholstered furniture and covered wagons.

Jute defined Dundee, and it is still the legacy from which the city fights to escape. In 1901, out of a total population of 160,000, 45,000 people or almost half of the working population worked directly in textile production while thousands more were involved in the ancillary industries which supported the trade; bobbin-turning, shuttle manufacture, textile engineering. Three-quarters of those directly involved in manufacturing textiles were women, who were employed alongside teenage boys and children under the age of 14. In 1896, 2,793 children were employed in mills under the iniquitous half-time system, by which children could be employed, usually as shifters, for 6 hours a day if they attended school for the other 'half day'. Dundee was the last city in Scotland to abolish half-time working. The employment of women and children kept wages depressed and kept men out of employment. At the turn of the century a man who worked in the mills, unless a foreman or an engineer, would not expect to earn enough to support a family, but if his wife and children worked as well they could earn enough to live on.

The factories which produced the jute were first established along the water sources needed to power the machinery, and clustered around the Hilltown, Dens and Blackness areas of the city. Many mills survive and have been variously adapted as flats, student accommodation, snooker halls, offices and industrial units.

Jute's heyday was before the First World War, followed by a period of steady decline interspersed with periods of recovery thereafter. The first jute mill in India opened in 1855 and by the 1880s Indian jute was threatening Dundee's overseas markets. After the Second World War Dundee's share of the world jute market declined steadily and the 1970s saw massive closures across the city. Those textile firms that survived diversified into polypropylene, and today textiles account for under 2 per cent of the workforce.

Trade stand of Dundee Chamber of Commerce, 1930s.

Parade float of Dundee Jute & Flax Workers Union, *c.* 1940, celebrating the abolition of half-time working in 1918.

Staff leaving Cox's Works, *c.* 1910. Cox's Works in Lochee was the largest jute works in the world, employing over 5,000 workers at its peak. Its 35 acre site was laid out on a grid pattern and included its own bleachworks, stables, machine shop, timber stores, half-time school and railway.

Hand weaving at Mid-Wynd Works. The woman is hand spinning yarn. The picture gives some idea of conditions experienced by workers in the first half of the nineteenth century. In the 1840s and 1850s, Mid-Wynd Works had only 3 to 4 handlooms, but when power loom weaving was introduced in the 1860s this rose to 60 looms.

Senior staff at the Bowbridge Works, 1863. The Bowbridge Mill was opened in 1857 by J. & A.D. Grimond. Back row, left to right: G. Dobbie, W. Duncan, J. Jeffrey, G. Deans, D. Mudie, W. Rae, D. Watt, D. Fyffe, W. Reid, 'Cocky' Rodgers, Robert Reid, T. Davidson, W. Chalmers. Front row, left to right: W. Webster, D. Bennet, D. Isles, W.P. Butchart, J. McKenzie, A.A. Philip, J. Scott.

Robert Doyle and Rachel Devine, officials of the Jute and Flax Workers Union, 1939. The Jute and Flax Workers Union was founded in 1906 and was unusual in that half its executive seats were reserved for women. Textile unions in the city were only ever partly successful in organising the workforce and after a disastrous 6 month strike and lock-out in 1923 the Jute and Flax Workers Union was unable to combat the rationalisation and lay-offs of the 1930s.

Jute weavers in party mood, Hillside Works, c. 1910. Official holidays were few, and since they were unpaid women often found themselves short of money in holiday periods.

Powerloom weaving in the 1950s. The more highly skilled weavers were always better paid than spinners.

Hackling jute by hand, Indian sub-continent. Although the first jute mills were opened in India in the 1850s they were often run by Dundee managers and engineers, even after Independence from Britain.

Jute being unloaded at the docks, *c.* 1950.

The warehouse of A. & S. Henry's, Victoria Road. Because of the extreme flammability of jute, jute works were built using metal and stone with little or no wood in the construction.

Feeding jute into a spreader, 1950s. At this stage the raw jute was sprayed with a mixture of oil and water. It was then carded or combed to clean and straighten the fibres.

The carded jute or sliver was drawn at least two or three times before being spun. The final drawing added a crimp to strengthen the sliver for spinning. Crimping machines replaced the earlier roving machines which added a final twist to the sliver.

Hank winding jute yarn on to spools, c. 1950. The spools carried the thread for the warp thread in weaving.

Spinning and reeling floor, Ward Mills, Brown Street, before the First World War. Spinning was a dirtier occupation than weaving because of the fine particles or 'stour' which were released into the atmosphere during the spinning process.

The woman on the right is spinning twisted sliver from a roving machine on to bobbins. The woman on the left is winding yarn from the bobbins on to cops, which would then be fitted into the shuttle to provide the weft thread for weaving.

Ingiver (right) and drawer (left) setting up a loom. The warp threads from the beam at the back are threaded through the heddle and knotted by hand.

Weaving flat, Douglas Mill, Douglas Street, 1919. Built in 1835, the mill is still in use as industrial units.

General view showing the enormous size of a weaving flat at Baxter Brothers' Dens Works. Baxter's was one of the largest firms in Dundee. The Lower Dens Mill was built in 1822, processing flax for coarse linens, followed by the Upper Dens Works in 1826. The firm was unusual in that it did not convert to jute production but stayed with linen until it closed in 1980.

Weavers at Nelson Street Works, *c.* 1910. While many thousands were employed at the largest works, some factories ran with only a handful of staff.

Weaving bags on a circular loom, 1950s. The beams on either side fed the loom and as the bag was woven it dropped to the floor below.

One of the great calenders in operation. Calendering involved the finishing of cloth by running it through large steam rollers to give the cloth a smooth finish.

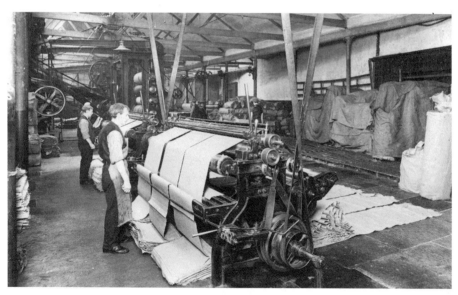

Cropping cloth. The cropping machines sheared off surplus fibres from the cloth and, in this case, folded it. Men were largely concentrated in preparing and finishing work in the jute industry, leaving spinning and weaving to the women.

Printing sacks, A. & S. Henry's, 1924. A. & S. Henry's, a Manchester-based textiles firm, opened a Dundee branch in 1858 specifically to manufacture and print jute bags and sacks. They later expanded into spinning and weaving. With their magnificent premises in Victoria Road they became one of the city's major jute firms.

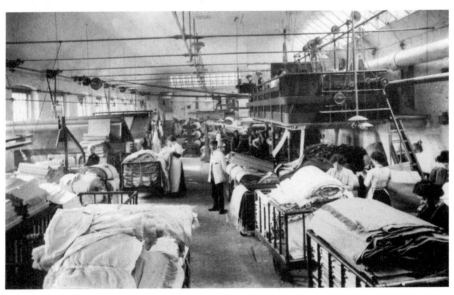

The Despatch Room, Baxter Brothers, 1890s. The white-coated 'gaffer' or foreman can be seen in the centre. An overseer at this time might earn 30s (£1.50) per week, the women and boys he supervised between 11 and 14s (55p–70p) per week. Relations between female workers and male gaffers were often poor.

Machinists sewing sacks, *c.* 1950.

Fire Brigade, Polepark Jute Works. Because jute was so flammable and the local fire service poorly developed, many of the jute firms employed their own fire brigades.

Despite their fire-proof construction blazes at jute works were fairly common. This fire at the Perth Road premises of Wm Lawson and Sons' Tay Rope Works in June 1900 forced the evacuation of neighbouring tenements, but the heavy fire-proof doors and hydrants at the works, together with the fire brigade, saved the premises.

Polepark Works Fire Brigade fire drill, *c.* 1900.

Bowbridge Works Fire Brigade, 1941. Grimond's was the first firm to introduce works fire brigades in the 1890s. Bowbridge and Maxwelltown had their own pumped water supply from a 240 ft deep well at Bowbridge Works.

T.L. Miller, Managing Director, and his Works Manager in the Managing Director's Office, Hillside Jute Works, 1911.

The engine room at Hillside Jute Works. The looms, spinning frames and other works machinery were driven by belts linked to overhead power shafting, which was in turn powered by great steam engines like the one above.

Ramesh Sharma, spinner at the South Anchor Works, West Hendersons Wynd, *c.* 1965. The higher wages paid in light engineering firms led to a shortage of spinners. Indian textile workers, many from the textile towns of Yorkshire, moved to the city for work in the 1960s.

The clerical staff of J. & A. D. Grimond's jute works, 30 March 1907. The staff includes: John S. Ramsay (Carpet Order, Clerk Head Office), G. Patterson (Clerk, Mill Office), John Rodgers (Apprentice Clerk, Mill), J.H. Macfarland (Cashier, Head Office), J. Johnson (Apprentice Clerk, Mill), A.A. Taylor (Clerk, Hessian Dept), A. Melville (Apprentice Clerk, Mill), John Goodfellow (App. Clerk, Maxwelltown Works), John S. Watson (Clerk, Head Office), Wm Smith (Clerk, B.B. Calender), Robt Smith (Book keeper, Head Office), Jas Guthrie (Clerk, B.B. Calender), John McQueen (Clerk, P.L. Factory), Alex Miles (Clerk, B.B. Calender), Robt Mains (Clerk, Head Office), Miss A.M. Dewar (Typist, Head Office), Ken D. White (Clerk, Head Office), Miss J.E. Stowell (Typist, Head Office), Alex C. Campbell (Yarn Order Clerk, Head Office), Miss A.L. Coyle (Typist, Head Office), Will C. Gow (Twine salesman, Head Office), David Fraser (Clerk, Maxwelltown Works), Will G. Fair (Yarn salesman, Head Office), Lindsay Keith (Clerk, Head Office), A.S. McKenzie (Hessian salesman, Head Office), Wm Laird (Clerk, Maxwelltown Works), Wm Swann (Sec. and Treasurer), Chas Kelly (Designer, Maxwelltown Works), L.G. Macintyre (Joint Managing Director), A.O. Thompson (Clerk, Mill Office), Wm Strange (Telephone Exchange, Head Office), John Phin (Clerk, Mill Office), Geo. Kirk (Engineer, B.B. Works), David Robertson (Clerk, Mill Office), Andrew Reid (Clerk, P.L. Factory), Robt Taylor (Clerk, Mill Office), Mr Charles Pearson (Manager, B.B. Works), J.S.R. Smith (App. Clerk, Mill Office), John White (Manager, B.B. Works), Wm Cowper (Clerk, Mill Office), E.C. Gib (Manager, Maxwelltown Works), H. Laird (Manager, Head Office), W.C. Smith (Spinning Manager, B.B. Works), J.C. Crammond (App. Clerk, B.B. Calender), Robt Reid (Factory Manager, B.B. Works), Geo Mooney (Office Boy, Mill Office), James Wallace (Clerk, B.B. Calender), F.F. Robertson (App. Clerk, Head Office), C.W. Crosby (Designer, Maxwelltown Works), David Brown (App. Clerk, Head Office), Robt Grieve (Shipping Clerk, Maxwelltown Works), W. Chalmers (App. Clerk, Mill Office), Jas Anderson (Carpet Salesman, Head Office), H.F. Slidders (Twine Order Clerk, Head Office), J.S. Kerr (Cashier, Mill Office)

Tenters and undertenters at the Tay works, 1912. Tenters were the mechanics who repaired the looms in the factory. Exclusively male, highly unionised and comparatively highly paid, they were frequently hated by the weavers who, paid on piece-work rates, were totally dependent on their skills to keep the looms going.

'The Biggest Heald ever made in Scotland' was produced by Messrs Thomas Miln & Co. in 1965.

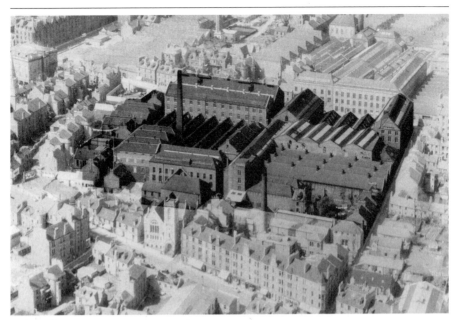

Aerial view showing Mid-Wynd Works, 1957. Mid-Wynd was a large works for the weaving and finishing of cloth. A mill stood on the site from 1797 until the complex was demolished in 1980.

Dinner hour at the Caldrum Works. When the 'bummer' or hooter sounded workers could be seen pouring out of factory gates across the city. Most workers lived close enough to their work to go home for lunch. For women it was often an opportunity to feed the baby left with grannie or prepare the evening meal before racing back to the mill.

Mrs Catherine Millar, trainer, and trainee weavers, Sidlaw Industries, *c*. 1965.

Staff and children at Baxter Brothers' nursery, 1955. With a largely female workforce Dundee jute works were of necessity amongst the first in the country to run peace-time crèches for employees.

Mrs Ann Ransford's retirement presentation, Hillside Works, c. 1970. Mrs Ransford was over 80 at the time.

Staff at the Douglas Street Works, 1920s.

Pipe Major Harry Watson pipes himself out of Baxter Brothers Upper Dens Works after 56 years as a lodge boy, apprentice engineer, engineer and foreman.

Jute and hemp were used to produce rope in rope works throughout the city. Two of the biggest, Tay Rope Works and the Dundee Rope Works, stretched between the Perth Road and Magdalen Green and were partly in the open air. There were also smaller rope works on the Hilltown.

The ropewalk in Wm Lawson & Sons' Tay Rope Works in Thomson Street, before 1920. The walk was 1,050 ft long and was demolished in 1985.

Women employed in coiling and packing fine cordage and twine.

Millwrights' shop, Wm Lawson & Sons' Tay Rope Works, Thomson Street.

Moving rope on the Perth Road.

Section Three

ENGINEERING AND SHIPBUILDING

The launch of the SS Iceland, 30 April 1943. Ships were normally paid for in three instalments, the first when the order was placed, the second after the launch and the third after sea-trials.

As a textile centre and port it was inevitable that engineering in Dundee would develop two main strands; the production of textile machinery and shipbuilding.

These industries developed in the late 18th and early 19th centuries in riverside sites to the east of the town centre. Many sites established then, such as the Dundee Foundry, Lilybank Foundry, Douglas Foundry and Ward Foundry, were to exist for the next 150 years.

If women dominated the textile industry, engineering was an entirely male preserve dominated by craft unions and providing relatively stable and well-paid work to some 25 per cent of the workforce. Major engineering firms in the city included Urquhart, Lindsay & Company, Robertson and Orchar, Charles Parker, Thomas C. Keay and, just outside the city boundary, J.F. Low of Monifieth.

Dundee was prominent in the development of steam ships and almost all the Dundee firms specialised in them. The city's major shipbuilders were Gourlay Bros, until its closure in 1909; Alexander Stephens (1844–93) who produced many of the whalers for the Dundee fleet; its successor, Dundee Shipbuilders; and W.B. Thomson's Caledon Shipyard.

Apprentice shipwrights at the Panmure Yard. Shipwrights served a seven-year apprenticeship. When time-served they were the aristocrats of the yard, earning high wages but facing lay-offs in periods of slump.

The Caledon Shipyard, 1939. W.B. Thomson of the Stobswell Tay Foundry moved into shipbuilding in 1874 with an order from the Earl of Caledon, after whom the new yard was named. It specialised in small to medium-sized steamships and, after a merger with Henry Robb of Leith, as Robb-Caledon became the only local yard to survive after the First World War. For the next sixty years it supplied luxury liners, naval cruisers, merchant ships, ferries, aircraft carriers and bulk-cruisers until its closure in 1983.

Traction engine crane, Caledon Shipyard, Stannergate, *c.* 1910.

The launch of SS *Discovery*, 21 March 1901 at Dundee Shipbuilders, by Lady Markham, wife of Sir Clements Markham, President of the Royal Geographic Society. The specially built ship, with its triple-skinned hull intended to withstand ice, was based on the design of Dundee whaling ships and was rigged with sails made from Baxter Brothers' famous Dundee sail-canvas.

The pipe bending shop at the Caledon Shipyard, early 1930s. Heating coils for a motor tanker can be seen in the foreground.

Workers coming off shift at the Caledon. From left: Roy McKelvie, John Robertson, Rab Smith and Tom Elder.

Hendry Ross, patternmaker, turning a pattern for a ship's propeller.

The carved limewood pattern for the ship *City of Dundee*, launched in 1961. A replica of the ship's badge made from this pattern now hangs over the entrance of the City Chambers.

The prefabricated bow of the *Athel Prince* cargo boat being raised in position, 1959.

Shipyard workers fitting out a ship at the Stannergate, 1960s.

Slipway, Caledon, 1930s.

The MV *Charon*, built by Robb-Caledon in 1936 as a passenger and cattle ship for Alfred Holt & Company. All the Caledon-built ships for Holt's were given Greek names, often taken from classical mythology.

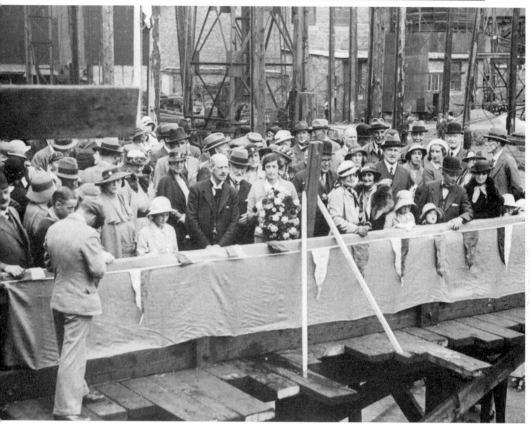

Miss Hilda Cowper launches the motor-coaster *Arbroath*, 14 August 1935. The *Arbroath* was built for the Dundee, Perth and London Shipping Company.

Women workers, Caledon Shipyard, 1918. During the First World War women workers were welcomed into the shipyards only to find the gates firmly closed after the war ended. The same thing happened in 1939–45, and it was not until the equal opportunities legislation of the 1970s that women were finally admitted as full-time workers in the shipyards.

The Lilybank Ragtime band, 10 August 1918. Engineering workers at the Lilybank Engine works raised £500 for wartime charities with their fancy dress parade. The men's costumes included nurses, witches, explorers, schoolchildren and soldiers.

Building a 90 ton rope fly-wheel in a pit, J. & C. Carmichael's Ward Foundry, 1920s. J. & C. Carmichael's was founded by the famous engineers James and Charles Carmichael of Glasgow in 1810 in the West Ward Foundry, later Ward Foundry, in Guthrie Street. In the early days they had a shipyard at the Seabraes and supplied steam boat engines and the engines for the locomotives of the early Dundee and Newtyle Railway. The firm came to specialise in machine tool production and engines and boilers for the Dundee textile trade. It closed in 1929.

The fitting shop staff at James Carmichael & Co., Guthrie Street, 1923.

Fitter David S. Kidd stands by a crankshaft made for the Victoria Jute Mills, Calcutta.

Loading and delivering electrical machinery made by the firm of Sturrock and Murray, 1940s.

Sturrock and Murray were founded in 1913 by R.F. Sturrock and Peter Butchart Murray. Their order books show that they supplied a huge variety of equipment to firms the length and breadth of Scotland and England.

Staff at Sturrock and Murray pose for a photograph after completing a major job. George Murray, Workshop Manager, is on the far right.

The Drawing Office of James F. Low & Co. Ltd, Monifieth. Low's specialised in producing jute machinery. In 1930 the foundry covered 15 acres and employed 700 men in the works and 60 in the offices.

STREET LIFE

Newspaper and periodical barrow outside the Royal Arch, Dundee docks. The original Royal

Arch was erected in 1844 for the visit of Queen Victoria and Prince Albert. It was designed

in wood as a temporary structure but was replaced by a stone arch in 1851. The crowd of

men behind may have been looking to be hired for casual work on the docks.

Most work today is carried on behind closed doors, but it was not always so; many people spent their working lives outdoors.

Much selling was done on the streets in the city's markets on High Street/Reform Street and the Greenmarket. The Greenmarket was held on Tuesdays, Fridays and Saturdays, and was a favourite trip out on Saturday evenings for families.

Street traders have virtually disappeared from modern streets but sold everything from cooked food to toys and flowers. Itinerant pedlars would knock at doors offering to sell clothes, mend pots, sharpen knives or remove rags.

Open air gatherings were much more common than today. Big public occasions were often marked by processions of workers from mills and factories carrying banners or tools and when the great depression hit the city in the 1930s it was on the streets that the unemployed were most visible.

Market stalls in the High Street with a view up Reform Street, 1860s.

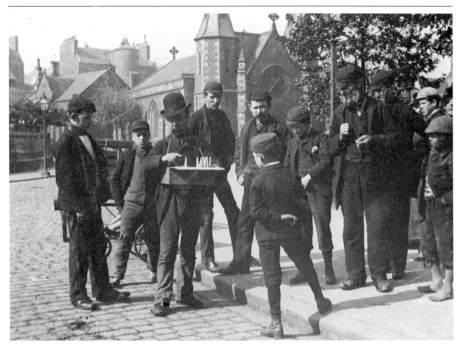

A street seller demonstrates what appear to be toys in Albert Square, *c*. 1900.

An organ grinder with a donkey and cart. The notice says: 'CHARMING BIRDS/FOR THE SMALL SUM OF ONE PENNY/FROM THIS BOX A PLANET/SEE FOR YOURSELVES.'

Open-air traders selling crockery and pots outside the Crown Hotel, 40 The Greenmarket. The Crown Hotel was on the corner of Shore Terrace, approximately where the Dundee District Council Housing Offices are today.

Luigi Coletta, ice-cream trader, with his barrow, 1907. Ice-cream was made fresh daily because of the lack of refrigeration facilities. After mixing his own ice-cream, a vendor would often push his barrow for miles for up to 12 hours a day to make a living.

New and second-hand stalls in the Greenmarket. The Greenmarket was a bargain-hunter's paradise with fish, meat, flower and sweetie stalls as well as new and second-hand household goods.

If you couldn't afford a newspaper advertisement a horse and cart could do the job almost as well.

Itinerant street preachers outside the Albert Institute. The hand barrow behind belongs to D. Meek & Son.

Refuse collection, 1920s. The refuse from house middens was shovelled into barrows, which were emptied out on the sides of roads to be collected by horse and cart.

John Cochrane McGowan and his dog Bess, *c.* 1940. John McGowan went blind at the age of 6 months after an attack of the measles. An accomplished accordionist, he was a familiar sight in the town. His favourite pitches were the Vaults (the old area to the south of the High Street) and Dens Park.

A horse-bus of the Dundee Tramway and Carriage Company, which was a private company from 1877 until it was taken over by the City Corporation.

Tram No. 55, which ran on the Strathmartine Road/Downfield route.

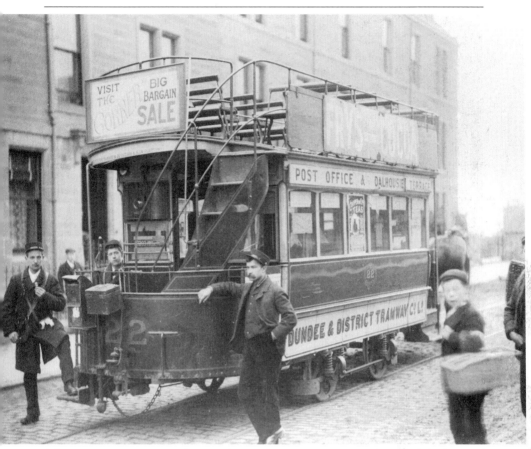

The City Corporation ran the tram service from 1 June 1899. It electrified the line and turned the system into one of the most efficient in the country. An extensive system of early morning workers' trams was run, as well as special cars to some works. This photograph shows the driver and conductor of tram No. 22. Fares between High Street and Ninewells were 2*d* (1p) inside and 1½*d* outside.

The Lady Mary Fair in the Greenmarket, Shore Terrace, *c.* 1915. The Lady Mary Fair was originally a medieval fair held on 15 August and is known to date back to at least the 13th century. It was traditionally held in the High Street but from 1907 was moved to Shore Terrace to avoid congestion. The last fair was held in 1933.

Lifeboat Saturday. Even after the RNLI took over the lifeboat at Broughty Ferry in 1861, the service was entirely funded by public donation. The annual parade and flagday through the Dundee streets was one of the most successful methods of fundraising and two of the crew of the boat can be seen leaning forward to catch donations thrown into their hats. The 'boat' was a full scale canvas replica in case the real vessel was required for a launch!

Demonstration in support of the Franchise Bill, Albert Square, 20 September 1884. Fire carts and banners for J. & A.D. Grimond's Bowbridge Works and Maxwelltown Works can be seen in the mid-ground while the group on the extreme right of the picture are carrying jute bales on sticks. Workers were often given time off to attend demonstrations in support of political causes favoured by works owners.

Unemployed protest march. The National Unemployed Workers Committees were a movement of the 'organised unemployed' in the depression years between the wars. Both nationally and in Dundee, Communist Party members were prominent. In September 1931 a series of local marches against the Means Test led to clashes with the police and several arrests.

Section Five

THE MILITARY

Colour Sergeant, 5th Company, 1st Forfarshire Rifle

Volunteers, 1860s. This photograph is from an

album presented to Henry Boase by members of the

Company in 1866. Boase, who was a lieutenant in

the 5th Company from 1859 to 1865, came from a

mill-owning family in Dundee.

The Volunteer movement was an enduring feature of the late Victorian and Edwardian army. It was a national movement which spawned local units for home defence in every British town. A significant number of young working-class men took part in the weekly activities of the Volunteer forces. In Scotland Volunteers were particularly active, with a much higher proportion of the population in the force than elsewhere in Britain.

Most Volunteers were amateur part-time soldiers participating in their leisure hours, but there were also a few regular soldiers seconded to the units. Skilled tradesmen were particularly valued in the Volunteer force because of their craft abilities.

After a number of organisational changes the Victorian Volunteer force survived, under a new name, to become the reformed Territorial force of 1908. In the same decade Dundee became more closely involved in military life, with the establishment of a branch of the Royal Naval Reserve in 1903 and the setting-up of a peace-time submarine base in 1909.

With the mass mobilisation of two World Wars, militarisation in the 20th century has made a deep and tragic impression on the city. In both conflicts thousands of young men fought for their country overseas, while at home thousands of men and women were conscripted to the industrial and defence effort.

Senior Officer, 1st Forfarshire Rifle Volunteers, 1870s.

Two officers of the Forfarshire Artillery Volunteers, 1870s. Unlike NCOs and other ranks, who were drawn from the upper working classes, Volunteer officers were from middle class and professional backgrounds.

Forfarshire Artillery Volunteers practise loading and firing their old-fashioned muzzle-loading guns at the Buddon Ness range (near Barry), early 1880s. The practice battery was established there in 1882.

Annual camp of the Tay Division Engineer Volunteers on Castle Green, Broughty Ferry, 1890. All Volunteer units had to hold an annual camp as part of their training and proof of their military 'effectiveness'. These were often held as close to the home town as possible and were open to the public to visit.

Left to right: Lieutenants W. Coyle and G.H.L. Boase, Major W.H. Fergusson (Commanding Officer) and Captain R.A. Fergusson of the Engineer Volunteers, 1891. They are on the harbour pier at Broughty Castle with two 'submarine' (i.e. underwater) mines. The purpose of laying a minefield at the mouth of the Tay was to prevent an attack by armed ships.

'Submarine Miners' Engineer Volunteers on board the *Admiral*, one of their two minelaying steam launches, 1896. First raised in 1877, the Volunteer Miners unit was expanded in the late 1880s. The War Department built an engineering depot (now demolished) next to Broughty Castle, bought the old railway harbour and provided special minelaying equipment, including the launches.

Officers of the Volunteer Miners outside Broughty Castle, 1896. Back row, left to right: Captains F.S. Stephen and E. Carmichael, Chaplain Revd H.M. Davidson, 2nd Lieutenants J.L. Garrick and J.A. Murdoch. Front row: 2nd Lieutenant C.F.L. Brown, Lieutenant J.H. White, Major W.H. Fergusson (Commanding Officer), Captain W. Coyle, Surgeon-Lieutenant G.O.C. Mackness, Quarter-Master J.H. Luis. Captain Coyle was a Royal Engineer regular, permanently seconded to the unit.

'Submarine Miners' Engineer Volunteers building a temporary bridge as an exercise during their annual camp in Broughty Ferry, July 1906. Ironically this highly skilled and specialised unit was disbanded in 1907, when mine defences in British ports were discontinued.

Lord F.S. Roberts (Commander-in-Chief of the British Army) visiting Broughty Castle, 19 August 1903, during a tour of Scottish regiments and military stations. After inspecting the submarine miners depot and the artillery battery, he boarded one of the mine-laying steam launches. Lord Roberts' tour came at a time when the usefulness of the Volunteers as a defence force was being discussed at a national level.

Colonel and Mrs Tyrie on an official visit to an Indian Maharajah, between 1911 and 1920. D.A. Tyrie, a Colonel in the Indian Army, was then Aide-de-Camp to the British Governor of Bengal. Brought up in Dundee, Tyrie had gone to India as a jute salesman in 1888. He retired in 1920 and returned to the city to live at St Helens on the Perth road.

NCOs and men of an Active Service Section, 1st (City of Dundee) Volunteer Battalion The Black Watch (formerly the 1st Forfarshire Rifle Volunteers), 1900. Nearly 300 local infantry volunteers saw service in the Boer War in South Africa (1900–2), either in Active Service Companies sent out by their Volunteer units, or by enlisting directly in the Army and Imperial Yeomanry.

Soldiers receiving machine-gun training on Castle Green, Broughty Ferry, early 1918. During the First World War a number of army units were quartered at Broughty Castle and in the residential district around Castle Green.

Submarine entering Dundee docks. The Royal Navy established a submarine base in Dundee's King William IV dock in 1909. The base's complement was 600 naval personnel.

HMS *Vulcan* and a submarine in the Tay. *Vulcan* was the parent ship and living quarters for Dundee's submarine base. The ship was anchored in the Tay by Newport.

Submarines moored on the south side of King William IV dock, *c.* 1912. In that year the base's flotilla consisted of HMS *Vulcan*, 12 submarines and the torpedo gunboat *Hebe*; there was usually a destroyer on hand as well.

Black Watch Reservists in front of Morgan Academy, probably between 1916 and 1918. In addition to the existing Territorial Battalions of the Black Watch, which were continuously expanded during the war, two new volunteer Battalions were specially created in Dundee. Military conscription from 1916 drafted men up to the age of 51 for various military service duties.

Men of the 4th Battalion ('Dundee's Own') The Black Watch embarking at Tay Bridge Station to go to the front, 23 February 1915. The 4th Battalion was a Territorial unit, raised solely in Dundee. They reached France on 26 February and suffered terrible losses at the Battle of Neuve Chapelle in March and at Loos in September, 1915.

Women munitions workers at Parker's Engineering Works, Balgray Street, Dundee. From the middle of the First World War men were conscripted to fight in the army and women were conscripted to maintain industrial production. Vast quantities of munitions were required to support the artillery barrages of trench warfare.

Platoon of Black Watch Reservists, taken on Àrmistice Day, 11 November 1918. Throughout the First World War reserves were raised, mobilised for home defence duties and reduced as men were drafted to replace casualties at the front. Altogether over 4,000 Dundonians were killed on active service during the war.

This photograph possibly shows a First World War recruitment parade in Dundee's High Street. The soldiers to the right of the platform of civic dignitaries are wearing battledress, with khaki covers over their kilts.

Portrait of John Alexander, one of 16 Dundonians killed fighting the Fascists in the Spanish Civil War. More than 120 men from Dundee went to fight with the International Brigades supporting the Republican government forces. John Alexander was a railwayman and unmarried. Apparently he went to Spain in place of his friend, John Molloy, who was married with children. Two months after arriving he was killed.

Fire-watch team training at the Polish Engineering Cadet School, Tay Street School, c. 1940. Polish soldiers were stationed in and around Dundee, Angus and Fife building and manning coastal defences. Later in the war they were moved away to regroup and train for the invasion of Europe.

Members of a civilian (Auxiliary Fire Service) fire-fighting team at Hillside Works. The Auxiliary Fire Service was a national volunteer organisation, set up in anticipation of massive air-raids. Dundee was virtually unscathed with 38 bombs dropping on the city, causing little damage and only 3 civilian fatalities.

Senior officers of 2nd Dundee Battalion, the Home Guard, outside the offices of the Territorial Army Association, *c.* 1944. The Home Guard, made up of men (and men only) not required for military service, numbered nearly 5,000 in Dundee in 1944. They were used extensively for home defence duties. In the later stages of the war the 2nd Battalion manned the Castle Green battery at Broughty Ferry.

Promotion display for salvage collections in Dundee, part of the national salvage drive during the Second World War. By August 1940, 789 tons of salvage had been collected in the city. Some of the salvage collections were simply to make civilians feel involved in the war effort – aluminium pots and pans were collected, supposedly for making aeroplanes, and then stockpiled. However, rags, food scraps, glass and paper *were* all successfully recycled.

Section Six

A HEALTHY CITY

Two young domestic servants wearing the familiar cap and apron. Relatively few women worked in domestic service. In 1911 only 5.8 per cent of Dundee working women were in service compared to 29 per cent in Edinburgh and 18 per cent in Aberdeen. This partly reflected opportunities in textiles but also reflected the lack of middle class homes in the city. Most people were too poor to employ anyone else.

The massive growth of the textile industry led the city's population to quadruple between 1821 and 1881 while little new housing, sanitation or infrastructure were added to an essentially medieval city. Accommodation was hard to find. Rents were commonly a fifth of the average wage, most families lived in two rooms, while others rented a room or even part of a room from another family. In 1901 Dundee had the highest rates of overcrowding, infant mortality and wife beating in Scotland. Dundee had more public houses per head of population than other towns while poverty, poor cooking facilities and large numbers of working women led to an appalling diet based around tea with sugar and bread. The average height of 11 year old Dundonian boys was 4½ inches less than that of 11 year old boys from Angus.

The second half of the 19th century and the first half of the 20th century were spent in a struggle to reverse the appalling social conditions brought by industrialisation, first by private charitable means and latterly by local authority and government agencies.

Orphanages, hospitals, nurseries and homes for the elderly were mostly provided by religious and charitable trusts. Many, such as the Free Breakfast Mission and free school meals, were concerned with simply feeding people.

Dundee Social Union, an influential group at the turn of the 20th century, set up the first restaurants for nursing mothers in Britain in 1906 and the Town Council set up similar establishments in 1909. The Town Council increasingly used its powers to improve the city environment, laying roads, piping water to the city from Lintrathen Reservoir in 1874, laying a network of sewers and demolishing the rabbit warren of city centre buildings which harboured infectious diseases such as typhoid. In the 1920s Dundee led the way in slum clearance and the building of local authority homes, but the pace and quality of improvements could not be maintained through the depression years that followed.

The children of P.S. Mudie, jute spinner and manufacturer, their friends and governesses, in the garden of their house The Hollies in Broughty Ferry.

Nurse and charge. Some very wealthy families had their own nursemaids; others hired private nurses as required from Dundee Royal Infirmary.

Midwife and newly born Margaret Pirie in the living room of a tenement flat in Stirling Street, 1922.

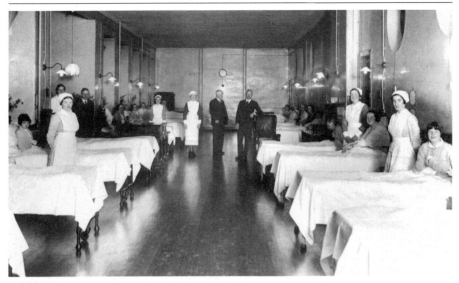

Ward 2, Dundee Royal Infirmary, on the day of the visit of HRH Prince George, 30 November 1933. DRI was Dundee's biggest hospital. First founded in 1782, the present premises were opened in 1855. The hospital was run by a board of governors and relied heavily on the generosity of local jute barons such as Mrs George Gilroy, who built a nurses home, or J.K. Caird, who funded the maternity hospital in 1899 and a cancer ward in 1907.

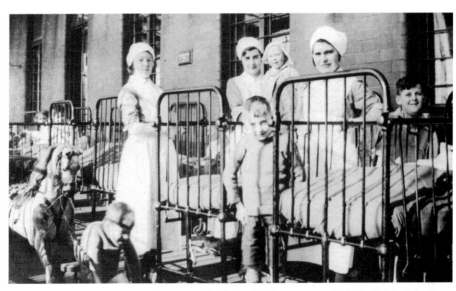

Nurses and patients on Ward 18, Dundee Royal Infirmary, c. 1930. Individual beds as well as wards were funded by subscription and often carried plaques bearing the name of the person who had sponsored the bed. DRI became part of the National Health Service in 1948.

Off-duty nursing staff relax outside Kings Cross Hospital chalet annexe. Kings Cross was opened as Dundee's infectious diseases hospital in 1890. It was voluntarily funded.

The opening of Duncarse House children's home in the Perth Road, 1 May 1924. The home was run by Dundee Combination Parish Council and was opened by Lady Helen Leslie MacKenzie.

Officers/Instructors of the Tay Training Ship *Mars*, *c.* 1900. The *Mars* was moored in the Tay from 1869 to 1929 as a school for difficult, delinquent or orphaned boys. It gave boys up to the age of 16 a craft, naval training and basic education. The regime was often tough and instructors were not above beating the boys in their charge.

Students at University College, Dundee, *c.* 1907. University College was founded in 1883 with financial support from the Baxter family. Only the children of the well-off could afford higher education, and they were guaranteed professional jobs as a result.

The Technical College which succeeded the Technical Institute (founded in 1888 with money bequeathed by Sir David Baxter) was heavily influenced by the needs of local industry, training textile engineers, architects, joiners and plumbers. Evening classes for workers seeking to improve their qualifications were as important as full-time courses.

Staff at Ancrum Road Primary School, 1930s. Dundee was the last Scottish city to have its own teacher training college, only setting one up after the First World War. Before that date teachers were provided by a local Committee for Training Teachers or by local churches.

Sandy Anderson, Hall Keeper for the Mission, 15 Hilltown, and companion.

Dundee Steeple bellringers. Back row, left to right: D. Goldie, W.C. Tasker, J. Berrick, R.A. Gibson, A. Strachan, D. McIntosh (conductor). Front row: J.B. Scott (Steeple Keeper), J. Knight. Inset: Kirkmaster A.L. Ramsay.

Louisa Malcolm Stevenson in her Salvation Army Uniform, *c.* 1920. The Salvation Army is one of the most enduring Christian charitable agencies in the city. Its lodging house, the Metropole, was complemented by the anti-alcohol work it carried out in the city in conjunction with the Gospel Temperance Union, Band of Hope, Good Templars and Rechabites.

The Revd A.R. Fraser of the Free Church of Scotland speaking at the first Robert Annan annual open air service, 6 October 1934. Robert Annan (1834–67) was a Dundee evangelist who died saving a boy from drowning in the Tay. He was commemorated by a stone in Annan Terrace marked 'Eternity', and the place was one of regular pilgrimage. In 1933 an appeal raised enough money to repair the Eternity stone, to publish his life story and to organise an annual open air service.

William Smart Atkinson, fireman, Dundee Fire Brigade, outside his house which was part of the New Central Fire Station in West Bell Street, *c.* 1905.

Dundee Fire Brigade engine pictured in West Bell Street outside the Sheriff Court, 20 July 1917.

Dundee Fire Brigade, West Bell Street Fire Station, *c.* 1909. The permanent staff at this time numbered eighteen, having recently risen from just eight!

Dundee Police Black Maria outside the Sheriff Court. The driver is D. McIntosh and Constable J. Cruikshanks stands to the rear. In 1911 the Dundee force was made up of 225 constables and officers.

PCs Alick Reynolds and John Tosh (Big Toshie) in their Alvis two-seater police car.

Practising traffic control, *c.* 1930.

Limewashing of houses, 1920s.
Limewashing was carried out partly
for visual, partly for hygiene reasons.
The Dundee Public Health Dept also
carried out the disinfection of beds,
mattresses, rugs, blankets, sheets,
clothes and the interiors of houses.

Horse drawn refuse collection wagon, 1920s.

Street cleaners outside the City of Dundee's Cleansing Department premises in Dock Street, 1930s. The wagon, which was used to collect street refuse, was steered by a tiller instead of a steering wheel.

Paper salvage at Foundry Lane. Paper salvage (along with the salvage of fabric and clothing) began in Dundee before the Second World War, motivated not by environmental fears but by the cash that could be received by sorting waste. Here two women are placing pre-sorted paper into a baling machine.

Delivering new bins, 1930s. The Dundee Corporation supplied every Council property with galvanised steel bins. Bins were also sold to private landlords and a dustbin maintenance scheme was run until the 1980s.

Caldrum Street Steamie, 1956. Washing facilities in most Dundee flats were inadequate to cope with the weekly wash load. There were six municipal wash houses, which were eventually closed as domestic washing machines became more widespread. Municipal launderettes were opened in their place but were never regarded with the same affection as the steamies, which were thought of as great places for a gossip.

CONSUMING

PASSIONS

Bell & Son Clothiers, 10 High Street, decorated to mark the coronation of

King Edward VII, 1902.

For large parts of British society, though not for all, real living standards have gradually risen throughout the twentieth century. This has inevitably meant greater demand for material things – from 'necessities' like clothes and furniture to 'luxuries' such as toys and cinema tickets. Compulsory education (since 1872 in Scotland) also stimulated a demand for books and magazines.

Over the last century every British city, no matter how poor or depressed, has produced a variety of consumer goods for local and national markets. Dundee was no exception. In 1930, as well as the staples of jute manufacture, jam-making, engineering and printing, Dundee could boast an assortment of manufacturing firms making, to name but a handful of products, furniture, cigarettes and tobacco, fizzy waters, fishing rods, paint, paper, bedding, brushes, window blinds, boots, shoes and underwear.

After the Second World War, Dundee entered a new phase, playing host to the UK manufacturing depots of global concerns such as Timex and NCR. The impact of the world economy was felt increasingly at a local level, as jute and shipbuilding went into steep decline. Local firms also became involved on a wider stage – Keiller's were bought out by Nestlé in the 1960s and Valentine's became a subsidiary of John Waddington's in the same decade.

Workman stirring the vats of lime used in skin and fur preparation at the Arctic Tannery in Marine Parade, c. 1913. The appalling smell from the tanneries pervaded the town and led to many calls for their removal from the city centre.

Potter's shoe shop, 12–16 Murraygate. Potter's were at various addresses in the Murraygate from 1866, when they were described as bootmakers, until 1974. With a luxurious interior, Potter's was thought to be quite an upmarket shop.

Cobblers at Potter's shoe repair business at 2 Meadow Entry. A pair of well-made shoes was expected to last for years and it was usual for shoe-shops to offer a repair service to customers.

David Drysdale produced high quality leather and tack goods, and was an example of how a Dundee firm could draw on custom from the surrounding countryside.

Turning chair legs at East Brothers' factory, South Road, Lochee. Francis East, a chair maker from High Wycombe, opened a factory in Clepington Road. Two of his sons set up their own business in 1895 in Albert Street, opening new premises in South Road, Lochee in 1911. They employed about 120 staff.

Polishing a chest of drawers, Lochee Cabinet Factory. East Brothers produced goods for the 'middle market' and supplied local shops such as Justice's, Robertson's, Buist, Forbes, Gillies, and Malcolm's as well as firms in Edinburgh and Aberdeen. Their main product was, surprisingly, lavatory seats made from imported South African hardwood, which were exported all over the world.

Members of the Dundee Branch of the Scottish Painters Society, 1913. Many of the early trade unions evolved from Friendly Societies and trade associations. It is interesting to note that the chairman appears to be wearing a kind of ceremonial apron.

The staff outside the premises of T.M. Sparks, bookbinder, at 2–4 Peter Street, 1908. The firm had moved to larger premises at 12–14 Peter Street by 1911 and branched out into printing under the name of the Croswell Press.

The despatch room at the Westfield Works of Valentine's. Valentine's of Dundee began as a one-man photography firm in the 1850s. By the turn of the century they were one of Britain's largest greetings card manufacturers with a workforce of 600 employees, mostly female, split between premises in the Perth Road and the Westfield Works. The firm closed its doors in the city for the last time in 1994.

The composing room, D.C. Thomson's Meadowside works, 1920s. Linotype operators can be seen setting the type in the background, and in the foreground a page is being assembled and clamped.

Reporters' room, D.C. Thomson, Meadowside, 1962. The publishers D.C. Thomson & Co. have been one of the town's most successful businesses for over 120 years. After taking over the *Dundee Courier* in the 1870s the firm merged with John Leng & Co., adding the *Dundee Advertiser*, the *Evening Telegraph*, *People's Journal* and *People's Friend*. The firm also has a lion's share of the children's comic market, and publishes teenage and women's magazines.

The Poets' Box bookshop in the Overgate, 1920s. Lowden McCartney is at the door.

Food, clothes and even a taxidermist could all be found in close proximity in the rabbit warren of streets behind the Overgate, *c.* 1913.

D.M. Brown's in the High Street. One of a number of large drapery 'emporia' which Dundee boasted before the First World War, Brown's was the grandest and most modern. It opened a tea-room in 1900 and a 400 ft long Arcade in 1908. The Arcade was an advertising display for the extensive wares of Brown's, rather than a mall of shops.

Dundee, never a rich city, had a thriving second-hand trade in the Greenmarket, which today is carried on in Dens Road.

The workforce of Alfred E. Powrie, rag, waste and metal merchant, 38 Seagate, 1922.

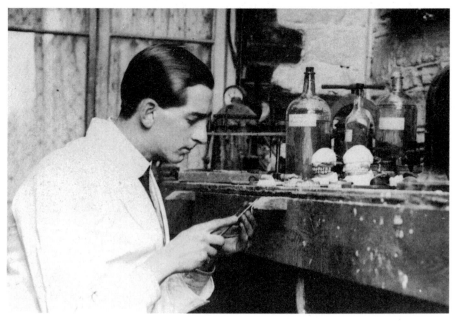

A dentist at work fashioning false teeth. Most dental surgeries and workshops were part of the dentist's home.

Davidson and Gray, wholesale chemists (with staff below), on the south side of the Nethergate, where the dual carriageway junction with Marketgait is today. The firm was one of the largest in Dundee and supplied the city's hospitals and many smaller chemists.

The staff of the American Roller Skating Rink in Melrose Terrace, Dundee, *c.* 1912. William Cowell, manager, is in the third row back, in the centre. Roller skating became a craze before the First World War. At one time Dundee had three rinks.

Mending skis in the ski department of Potter's Boot and Shoe Company.

Staff outing at Hamilton Carhartt's clothing manufacturers, *c.* 1950. The firm came to Dundee in 1942 and eventually employed 450 staff, mainly women, making overalls and workwear of all types.

NCR's Camperdown Factory, 1954. The National Cash Register Company based at Dayton, Ohio opened a factory at Camperdown in 1948. It rapidly became one of the city's largest employers.

Pinion-cutting parts for watch production, Timex, 1955. Timex too came to the city post-war, opening factories at Camperdown and Milton of Craigie. Wages were higher than in the mills and attracted many former mill workers.

Women workers at sub-assembly bench, watch production, in the Timex Camperdown Factory.

Dorothy Hutton, accounting machine operator, at the half-millionth machine made at NCR, 24 February, 1965. By 1965 NCR's factories had expanded to cover half the area of the Kingsway West Industrial Estate. The growth of the office and financial sector of the economy meant that 'the Cash' was ideally placed for meeting the markets of the future.

The shape of things to come: accounting employees of Henderson & Logie chartered accountants, 1968. Office work, formerly a small proportion of Dundee's working population, was by 1968 the most rapidly growing sector of the workforce.

Acknowledgements

First and foremost, thanks must go to the people of Dundee who have over the years donated their personal and family photographs to the museum: without their contribution there would be no book. Similarly, the museum has been allowed to copy many private photographs, some of which are reproduced here, and I would like to express my gratitude to the following organisations and individuals for permission to reproduce them: Allied Distillers Ltd (Stewart and Son), City of Dundee District Libraries, Mr H.M. East, Mrs F. Falaschi, Mrs G. Gierelo, Mr C. McDonald, Mrs I. Palmigiani, Mrs I. Ramsay, Mr H. Ross, Mr R. Sharma, Mrs M. Scott, Miss I. Shiell, D.C. Thomson and Co., Mr S. Urban and Mrs M. Young.

Secondly, I would like to thank my colleagues Gill Poulter, Rod Gordon and Jackie Arcari for their help in identifying photographs, and checking and typing the text. Especial thanks are due to David Stockdale for all his help with Sections One and Five and to Eileen Murison who worked so hard to produce the photographs. For all their help over years of enquiries, I would like particularly to thank Douglas Spence and the staff of the Photofiles Section at D.C. Thomson's.

Finally, thanks are due in no small measure to the City of Dundee District Council whose care over more than a century has collected and preserved these photographs for posterity and which has now made them available to a wider public.

The following photographs are reproduced courtesy of: D.C. Thomson & Co. Ltd, pp. 80, 90 (bottom), 110, 117, 123 (bottom), 125 (top); Dundee District Libraries, pp. 18 (top), 72 (bottom), 112; Mr Stewart Shaw, p. 125 (bottom).

BRITAIN IN OLD PHOTOGRAPHS

To order any of these titles please telephone Littlehampton Book Services on 01903 721596